MODERN WORLD NATIONS

AFGHANISTAN	IRAN
ARGENTINA	IRAQ
AUSTRALIA	IRELAND
AUSTRIA	ISRAEL
BAHRAIN	ITALY
BERMUDA	JAPAN
BOLIVIA	KAZAKHSTAN
BRAZIL	KENYA
CANADA	KUWAIT
CHINA	MEXICO
COSTA RICA	THE NETHERLANDS
CROATIA	NEW ZEALAND
CUBA	NIGERIA
EGYPT	NORTH KOREA
ENGLAND	NORWAY
ETHIOPIA	PAKISTAN
FRANCE	PERU
REPUBLIC OF GEORGIA	RUSSIA
GERMANY	SAUDI ARABIA
GHANA	SCOTLAND
GUATEMALA	SOUTH AFRICA
ICELAND	SOUTH KOREA
INDIA	UKRAINE

Australia

Terry G. Jordan-Bychkov
University of Texas, Austin

Series Consulting Editor
Charles F. Gritzner
South Dakota State University

CHELSEA HOUSE
PUBLISHERS
A Haights Cross Communications Company

Philadelphia

Frontispiece: Flag of Australia

Cover: Ayers Rock, Australia.

CHELSEA HOUSE PUBLISHERS

VP, NEW PRODUCT DEVELOPMENT Sally Cheney
DIRECTOR OF PRODUCTION Kim Shinners
CREATIVE MANAGER Takeshi Takahashi
MANUFACTURING MANAGER Diann Grasse

Staff for AUSTRALIA

EXECUTIVE EDITOR Lee Marcott
PRODUCTION ASSISTANT Megan Emery
SERIES DESIGNER Takeshi Takahashi
COVER DESIGNER Keith Trego
LAYOUT 21st Century Publishing and Communications, Inc.
Photos are all courtesy of Terry G. Jordan-Bychkov unless otherwise noted in Picture Credits

©2003 by Chelsea House Publishers, a subsidiary of Haights Cross Communications.
All rights reserved. Printed in China.

A Haights Cross Communications ⟡ Company

http://www.chelseahouse.com

First Printing

1 3 5 7 9 8 6 4 2

Library of Congress Cataloging-in-Publication Data applied for.

ISBN 0-7910-7609-1HC   0-7910-7771-3PB

Table of Contents

Australia

This rural ranch, or "station," as ranches are called in Australia, creates a pastoral setting near Batlow in the state of New South Wales. Australia has 11.5 percent of all sheep in the world.

1

Comparing Australia and the United States

A mericans find Australia both exotic and familiar. If you travel in Australia, many things will make you think you are still at home. At other times you will feel as if you are in some sort of a fantasy land.

HOW AUSTRALIANS ARE LIKE US

Americans can at once identify with a wealthy, English-speaking country with high living standards. Both Australia and the United States were colonized centuries ago by European immigrants, especially from the British Isles, settling a new continent across the seas. In both countries, the native people were brushed aside and decimated by disease and warfare. Both nations offered abundant natural resources and expanses of land for new farms, ranches, towns, and cities.

Nor should Americans find unusual a dominantly Christian country with a Protestant majority and sizable Roman Catholic minority. Also, both countries changed their immigration laws in the 1960s and 1970s to allow large numbers of Asians and other non-whites to enter and become citizens.

In size, the United States, with 3.7 million square miles (9.6 million square kilometers) of territory, resembles Australia, with 3 million square miles (7.8 square kilometers). The two countries even have similar shapes. Both are elongated east to west and span multiple time zones.

Popular Culture

The two countries share much in popular culture. Fast-food chains such as Pizza Hut, Kentucky Fried Chicken, and McDonald's appear in both lands. Australia has skyscrapers, automatic cash machines, neighborhood crime watch signs, and suburbs dominated by freestanding single-family homes. It has rodeos, self-serve gasoline (Australians call it "petrol") pumps, backyard barbecues, and department stores and grocery stores that are part of the same chains that are common in the United States.

Both Australia and the United States also make movies. Nicole Kidman, Toni Collette, Russell Crowe, Mel Gibson, and Paul Hogan are among the famous Australian movie actors. Australian stars in American films are not a new trend, though. The dashing 1930s movie star Errol Flynn was from the state of Tasmania.

Both countries call their currency the dollar and divide it into cents. Both are dominated by the automobile for personal transportation and have good highway systems complete with roadside parks. Both have shopping centers with names such as "Gateway Plaza." Both also struggle with drug addiction, teenage runaways, and juvenile suicide.

Sports

Like Americans, Australians love sports. Some of these games and activities we share in common—tennis, skiing, swimming, golf, yacht racing, surfing, camping, jogging, and hiking. Greg Norman from the state of Queensland has long been a colorful fixture on the professional golf circuit.

Sports also begin to reveal how Americans differ from Australians, however. For example, Australians have a much greater interest in horse racing than Americans do. Australian adults participate more in amateur sporting activities than Americans do. They play cricket instead of baseball and bowl on green lawns rather than indoor lanes. Australian football bears little resemblance to the American game—except in the level of violence. Basketball and ice hockey are both unimportant to Australians.

HOW AUSTRALIA IS DIFFERENT

The differences reach far deeper than sports. For one thing, Australia is the only country in the world to include an entire continent. Australia the country has the same territory as Australia the continent. Also, its population, only about 20 million, is one-fourteenth as large as that of the United States. This is mainly because most of Australia consists of deserts. It lacks the large expanse of fertile, well-watered land that has made America a "fruited plain."

Because of its much smaller population, Australia is divided into only six states—Queensland, New South Wales, Victoria, Tasmania ("Tassie"), South Australia, and Western Australia. A seventh administrative unit, the huge Northern Territory, has not yet become a state. In addition, the separate Australian Capital Territory (ACT)—the equivalent of the District of Columbia—houses the national capital, Canberra. It, too, lacks the status of a state.

Latitude

The United States lies mainly in the temperate middle latitudes, except for tropical Hawaii and subpolar Alaska. Australia, by contrast, has close to half of its land mass in the tropics, near the equator and north of the Tropic of Capricorn. In latitude, it is more like Mexico than the United States. In the state of Queensland, residents speak of "the tropical north."

Truly cold climates do not exist in Australia, which has no equivalent of Minnesota, Maine, or Montana, and it certainly has no Alaska. It does, however, possess lands like Florida, Texas, and even Hawaii. Tasmania resembles the Pacific Northwest.

Geographical Location

We also need to compare the geographical locations of the two countries. The United States is fairly close to Europe, across a relatively narrow ocean. Both Europe and North America are in the Northern Hemisphere, north of the equator.

By contrast, Australia is situated at the antipodes. That is, Australia is almost precisely at the opposite side of Earth from the British Isles and the rest of Europe, in the Southern Hemisphere. The very name "Australia" means "the southern land." The Australians, or "Aussies," say that they live "down under."

This means that summer and winter, spring and autumn, are reversed. Christmas and New Year's occur in early summer. The month of June marks the onset of winter. Americans may also find confusing the fact that the Pacific Ocean forms Australia's east coast.

The English, Irish, and other European pioneers who settled Australia journeyed much farther to find a new homeland than those who went to America. They went to an isolated continent in a far corner of the world. Europe for them was uncomfortably far away.

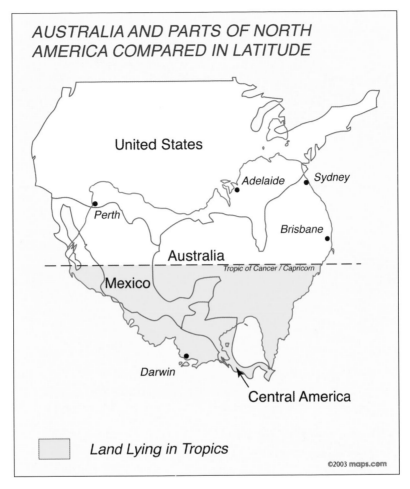

AUSTRALIA AND PARTS OF NORTH AMERICA COMPARED IN LATITUDE

United States

Adelaide   Sydney

Perth

Brisbane

Australia

Tropic of Cancer / Capricorn

Mexico

Darwin

Central America

Land Lying in Tropics

©2003 maps.com

A mirror-image map of Australia has been inverted and placed over a map of North America to show how the two continents compare in latitude. Close to half of Australia's land mass is located in the tropics.

The Habitat

The European settlers also found the native plants and animals of Australia very different from those they had known. Instead of forests of oak or pine, they found hundreds of kinds of eucalyptus, or "gum" trees. Instead of deer, bears, and beavers, they encountered completely exotic animals like kangaroos, koalas, wombats, and emus.

Speaking English

In this land of "Oz," a nickname Australians use for their homeland, the English language is somewhat different from that spoken in the United States. Pronunciation is much more nasal. Many Aboriginal words have been adopted, especially for towns, streams, animals, and plants. The result is place names such as "Coober Pedy," "Wagga Wagga," "Goondiwindi," and "Grabben Gullen." The last name, for example, means "small creeks" in the local Aboriginal language.

Everyday speech can also be confusing to Americans. *Ta* means "thank you;" a *billabong* is a flat-floored desert valley that sometimes floods; *brumbie* is a wild horse; *sultana* means "raisin;" a *sheila* is a woman; the term *road plant* alerts a driver to highway work ahead; a *roo bar* is a protective device on the front of an automobile that prevents radiator and headlight damage in collisions with kangaroos (they are not padded for the benefit of the kangaroo); and a livestock roundup is a "muster." One orders a "jug" rather than a "pitcher" of beer.

Aussies are also often more direct, if not blunt, in their speech and signs. In America, for example, one would never see official highway signs that read "slow down, stupid" or "if you drink, then drive, you are a bloody idiot"—but these exist in Australia.

Going Swimming

Australians love to swim. They have produced many Olympic champions. One stroke is even called the "Australian crawl." Swimming can be a bit different here, though. Swimmers should stay out of the water on the beautiful white tropical beaches near Darwin—a sting from the jellyfish there can kill a person. Swimmers also have to watch out for the huge saltwater crocodiles.

There are also guidelines to follow when using a swimming pool. A sign at the entrance to the public pool in the small Queensland town of Marlborough reads:

No topless or nude bathing.
No open wounds.
No urinating in pool.
No pushing.
No bombing.
No ball games.

Driving a Car

Aussies drive on the left side of the road, like the English. That is hardly the extent of the contrast with driving in the United States, however. Almost no freeways exist within city limits but instead are largely confined to rural areas. There are fewer red lights. Instead, drivers will often come upon "roundabouts"—traffic circles. The right-of-way belongs to cars already on the roundabout, and a driver must use the turn indicator to show whether he or she is still circling or is ready to exit.

In sparsely settled areas, one might encounter "road trains." These are truck cabs that pull up to five trailer rigs. Passing a road train can be very exciting.

One rule of the road in Melbourne states that if a driver wants to turn right at an intersection (the equivalent of a left turn in American traffic), he or she is supposed to get into the far left lane, out in the intersection, wait until the light turns amber, and then zip right across all the lanes. That rule is followed only in Melbourne—it would not be wise to try it in Sydney or any other city.

Eating Out

If a tourist wants something to eat while in Australia, he or she might just pop into a pizza parlor. Travelers should beware, however. Food choices can be very different in Australia compared to the United States. The Aussies will plop a fried egg on top of a pizza without so much as asking the customer.

Breakfast can be similarly unsettling. One should beware in particular of an innocent-looking spread for toast called "Vegemite." Made as a by-product of beer brewing, Vegemite gives the word *salty* an entirely new depth of meaning.

THE BRITISH EMPIRE

In spite of its remoteness, Australia has traditionally found its place in the British Empire. Though fully independent, it remains a British "commonwealth," like Canada. The queen or king of England is the nominal head of state.

Increasingly, though, Australia sees itself as an Asian-Pacific country. Its links to countries like Japan, China, India, and Indonesia have strengthened, as have trade ties to these lands. Many Asian immigrants have come to Australia. The ties to Europe have become more ceremonial and sentimental as they weaken.

Australia and the United States have long been allies, from the time of World War I. American troops fought alongside the Aussies in the Pacific during World War II, as well as in the Korean and Vietnam wars.

They also have become partners in the battle against Muslim extremist terrorism in the wake of the terrorist attacks on the United States on September 11, 2001. Australia is adjacent to Indonesia, the most populous Muslim country in the world. On October 12, 2002, more than 80 Australians were among those killed or injured when terrorists on the Indonesian island of Bali bombed a nightclub full of tourists in the town of Kuta. Before that horrible incident, Australians had thought their relative isolation sheltered them from terrorism.

AUSTRALIA IN REGIONAL CONTEXT

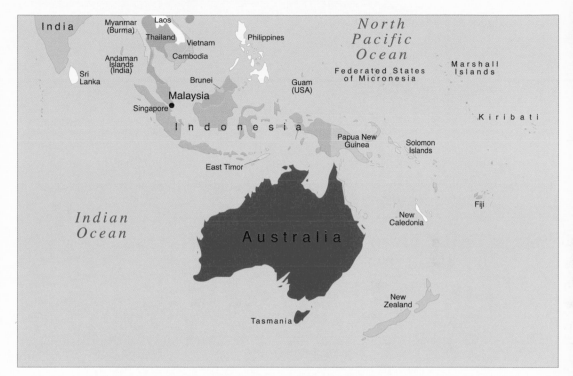

©2003 maps.com

Australia is the only country in the world that makes up an entire continent. The Pacific Ocean is off its east coast and the Indian Ocean is off its west coast. Because Australia is in the Southern Hemisphere, its seasons are opposite to those in the United States.

SOME THEMES FOR THE CHAPTERS AHEAD

With this introduction behind us, let's move on to a more detailed study of Australia. Ten major themes will dominate the chapters that follow: the continent-nation; Red Heart, Dead Heart; the Green Crescent; unique plant and animal life; Aborigines; Anglo-Celtic culture; Australia: one or many?; the "new" immigrants; city life; and "Bush" and "Outback" life.

Uluru (Ayers Rock), the famous Outback landmark, consists of red sandstone. The vast deserts that dominate the center of Australia give off a reddish hue and are called the nation's "red heart, dead heart."

2

The Australian Habitat

T he habitat—or physical geography—of Australia is unique and exotic. Immigrants from the British Isles found this new environment very different from anything they knew. Perhaps the biggest adjustment they had to make was to the climate. Not only were the seasons reversed, but the types of climate were largely unfamiliar to them.

RED HEART, DEAD HEART

The most outstanding feature of the Australian climate is the huge expanse of desert land, a "red heart, dead heart" dominating the center of the continent. Some people call Australia the "desert continent."

The word *dead* describes the desert character of the continental interior. *Red* comes from the mainly reddish hue of soil and rocks of these deserts. In fact, the color "signal" given off by the continent to orbiting satellite cameras is reddish, like the surface of the planet Mars. Another nickname for Australia is the "red continent." Aussies also refer to the "Red Centre" of their country.

Of course, the United States also has deserts. They are smaller and do not dominate the North American continent, however. If the broad semiarid zone that surrounds Australia's deserts were added to the red, dead heart, then the expanse of dry lands would take on gigantic proportions.

Outback and Bush

The Australians also use the word *Outback* in referring to the dry interior of the continent. One might also hear the term *bush*, but often that means essentially any rural area, including the Outback. Here, *bush* will be used to refer to the agricultural part of the land.

In the old days, crossing the desert Outback presented as many difficulties as getting across the famous Sahara Desert of Africa. Camels were introduced to Australia in imitation of the caravans of the Sahara. Much of the dead heart remains very difficult to travel even today, and the most effective mode of transportation is the small airplane, using countless dirt landing strips.

Water

In deserts, a lack of water is always the main problem. Relief is provided in several ways in Australia. First, the continent's only major river system—the Murray-Darling—flows as an "exotic stream" through much of the semiarid Outback in the southeast. An exotic stream is one that has its sources in rainy regions and then flows through dry areas on its way to the sea.

The other great source of water in the Australian Outback comes from artesian and other wells. Water is trapped under pressure, often at rather shallow depths. When wells are drilled, water rises to the surface. The largest source of such water is the Great Artesian Basin. Other shallow, subsurface water basins

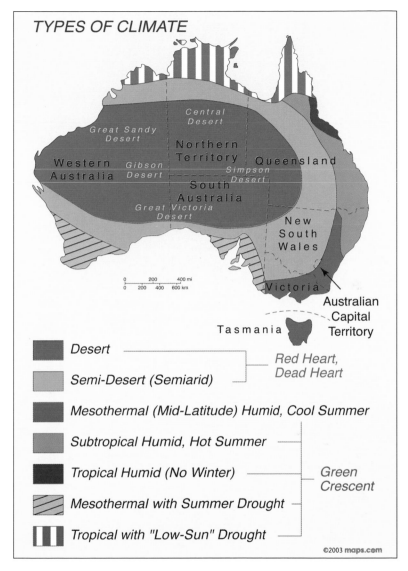

TYPES OF CLIMATE

Central Desert

Great Sandy Desert

Northern Territory

Queensland

Western Australia

Gibson Desert

Simpson Desert

South Australia

Great Victoria Desert

New South Wales

0   200   400 mi
0   200   400   600 km

Victoria

Australian Capital Territory

Tasmania

Desert ————————————— Red Heart, Dead Heart

Semi-Desert (Semiarid) ———

Mesothermal (Mid-Latitude) Humid, Cool Summer

Subtropical Humid, Hot Summer ———

Tropical Humid (No Winter) ————— Green Crescent

Mesothermal with Summer Drought —

Tropical with "Low-Sun" Drought ———

©2003 maps.com

In terms of climate, Australia is split between an expansive dry interior and a wet periphery called the "Green Crescent." The Green Crescent itself includes several climate types.

are not artesian and require pumps. American-style windmills do the pumping on many ranches.

Billabongs are, at least occasionally, still another source of water. These little flat valleys occur widely in the Outback.

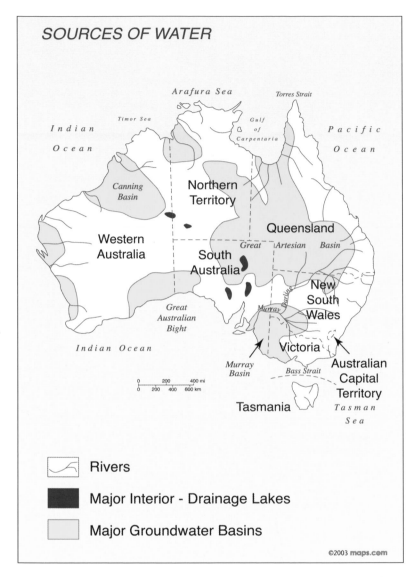

SOURCES OF WATER

This map shows the main rivers and groundwater basins of Australia. The exotic Murray-Darling river system and wells drilled in the Great Artesian Basin provide needed water to parts of Australia's dry Outback.

When rain does come, they quickly flood, due to their flatness. Even after the water evaporates, a good growth of grass survives. Some water remains below the sandy channels and can be reached by digging holes.

At one place in the mountains of southeastern Australia, a tunnel was bored through a ridge to divert water from the rainier east slope to the headwaters of the west-flowing Murray-Darling system. This allowed large irrigation projects in the interior.

In these ways, Australians have partially overcome the water shortage, providing irrigation for crops and ponds for livestock. Still, the water shortage remains a problem.

Fire

The other major problem of the dry Australian interior is the "bushfire." Fires, many of them set by lightning, repeatedly sweep across the deserts and semiarid regions. Fire is a natural part of the habitat.

The Aborigines also used fire to reduce brush and make hunting animals easier. When Europeans came to the dead heart region, though, and brought their herds and flocks of cattle and sheep, they began to try to suppress bushfires.

This created a problem. The vegetation became thicker. When the Bush did finally catch fire, enormous and very destructive blazes resulted. In recent decades, Australians have begun using small controlled fires. This technique removes the brush, encourages grass growth, and does not destroy livestock. Even so, major bushfires occur from time to time.

THE GREEN CRESCENT

On the south, north, and east, the dead heart is bordered by an encircling zone where adequate rainfall occurs. This "Green Crescent" includes several climate types. A subtropical humid climate dominates most of the eastern coastal area, a warm region with mild winters, hot summers, and rainfall during all seasons. This is the same climate found in the southeastern United States, in places such as Atlanta, New Orleans, and Dallas.

South of this, in the middle latitudes, lies the humid

The island state of Tasmania, in the humid temperate climate zone of Australia's Green Crescent, is said to have a climate similar to that of England. This photograph was taken near Sheffield, Tasmania.

temperate climate zone. Summers are relatively cool and winters mild. Here, and only here, did British immigrants find a mid-latitude moist climate similar to that of England. The island state of Tasmania is often said to have an English climate.

The southern and southeastern coasts also have a middle latitude temperate climate. Although they are dominantly humid, these areas experience a three-month drought in the summer season. They resemble Italy, Greece, or Southern

California climatically. Sometimes the seasonal drought lasts all year, with major consequences.

The Tropical North

Two distinctively tropical climates dominate the Green Crescent in northern Australia. One of these is a constantly wet and warm tropical humid climate, on the northeast Pacific coast of Queensland.

The other, more widespread tropical climate covers most of Australia's northernmost peninsula. It features a drought during the "low sun" half of the year. The term "low sun" is used instead of "winter," since the tropics have no cold or cool season, and instead remain warm year-round.

THE "BIG DRY"

Both the Red Heart and the Green Crescent periodically suffer drier than usual conditions. The worst drought in a century struck the continent in 2000 and had not yet broken by 2003. This "Big Dry," as the Aussies call it, greatly reduced production on farms and ranches. Sydney suffered reddish dust storms, and Melbourne, among many other cities, restricted the watering of gardens and washing of cars. Agricultural irrigation also was cut back.

Another result has been catastrophic bushfires in the Green Crescent. In 2002, one huge fire swept north of Sydney in New South Wales, all the way to the Pacific shore. In January 2003, a giant bushfire so fierce as to be called a "firestorm" entered the western suburbs of Canberra, the national capital. The fire killed four people and destroyed 400 homes. A resident of Canberra, Darrell Lewis, sent a dramatic e-mail message to this author entitled "A message from the burning capital of Oz," which chronicled the futile efforts of firefighters to turn back the fire. Fierce winds combined with the dry vegetation caused by the Big Dry made for a seemingly unstoppable fire. In his message, Lewis described the huge cloud of smoke and conveyed the fear felt by all Canberra residents.

TOO MUCH SUN

What happens when people from northwestern Europe move to a sunny, more tropical continent? Well, for one thing, they get a lot more skin cancer. Australians have the highest incidence of skin cancer of any people in the world. Most have fair skin, which developed after their ancestors lived for thousands of years in cloudy, northern lands. By contrast, the Aborigines, the native people of Australia, are very dark in complexion and are well adapted to the sunny climate.

Caucasians also develop eye cataracts at an alarming rate in Australia. This condition, too, is caused by sun exposure.

As if these problems were not enough, an "ozone hole" began developing about 1970 over the Southern Hemisphere. Air pollutants, especially from aerosol containers, destroy ozone at the upper levels of the atmosphere.

This ozone shields the earth surface from too much solar ultraviolet radiation. When the ozone shield thinned, Australians began getting skin cancer and cataracts at an even higher rate.

In response, the government has acted to reduce air pollution, though the problem is worldwide. Also, many school playgrounds have been roofed over, so that children no longer are exposed to the sun when outside. The problem is far from solved, however.

LANDFORMS

Australia has a fairly simple geographical pattern of terrain. In the east lies a very narrow and fragmented coastal plain. Strung like beads on a necklace, these small, separate lowlands are fertile and well watered. They are home to Australia's largest cities and most intensive agriculture. Examples include the Cumberland Plain, now largely filled by greater Sydney and the Hunter Valley, home of one of Australia's greatest vineyard districts.

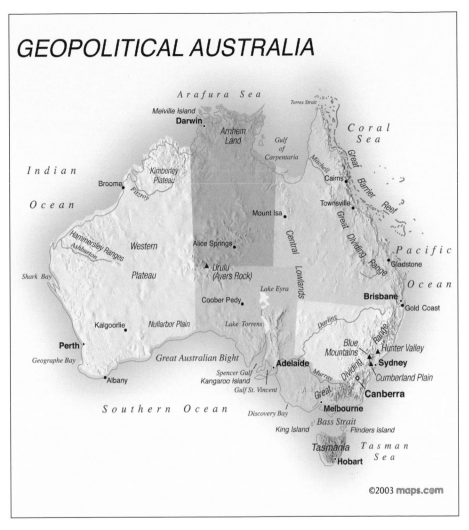

GEOPOLITICAL AUSTRALIA

A r a f u r a   S e a

Torres Strait

Melville Island

Darwin

Arnhem Land

Gulf of Carpentaria

*C o r a l
S e a*

I n d i a n

Kimberley Plateau

Broome

Fitzroy

O c e a n

Mitchell

Cairns

Great Barrier Reef

Townsville

Great Dividing Range

Mount Isa

Hammersley Ranges

Ashburton

Western

Alice Springs

Central Lowlands

P a c i f i c

Gladstone

Shark Bay

Plateau

Urulu
(Ayers Rock)

Lake Eyra

O c e a n

Coober Pedy

Brisbane

Gold Coast

Kalgoorlie

Nullarbor Plain

Lake Torrens

Darling

Perth

Blue Mountains

Range

Hunter Valley

Geographe Bay

Great Australian Bight

Murray

Dividing

Sydney

Adelaide

Cumberland Plain

Albany

Spencer Gulf
Kangaroo Island

Great

Canberra

Gulf St. Vincent

S o u t h e r n   O c e a n

Discovery Bay

Melbourne

King Island

Bass Strait

Flinders Island

Tasmania

*T a s m a n
S e a*

Hobart

©2003 maps.com

This map shows the entire territory of the nation – and continent – of Australia.

Great Dividing Range

Behind the small pockets of coastal plain we find the Great Dividing Range. In many places, it pinches out the plains and reaches the Pacific, forming a beautiful, rocky coast. The range is not one solid mass of mountains, but is instead a collection of separate ridges, ranges, and hill districts, each with a different name. Fertile, well-populated valleys lie between the different ridges.

The Australian Alps, which feature the country's only ski resorts, are seen here near the resort in Thredbo, New South Wales. The Alps are part of the Great Dividing Range, which forms Australia's Continental Divide.

The most impressive segment of the Great Dividing Range, the Australian Alps, includes Mount Kosciusko at 7,310 feet (2,228 meters), the highest peak on the continent. The Alps straddle the state border between New South Wales and Victoria. Australia's only ski resorts are here.

Also very beautiful are the Blue Mountains, west of Sydney. Although rugged, they are not as high as the Alps and normally have no snow. More typical of the Great Dividing Range are the Grampians in Victoria, which are really hills rather than mountains.

The Great Dividing Range forms Australia's Continental Divide, separating streams that flow to the Pacific from all

A eucalyptus scrub forest was removed to create a pasture here in northern New South Wales, in the Central Lowlands. The lowlands span Australia from south to north.

others. That may seem odd, considering how close to the east coast it lies.

Sometimes, the entire mountain zone is called the Eastern Highlands. That term allows inclusion of remote mountainous parts of Tasmania and eastern South Australia. The mountain scenery of Tasmania is among the most beautiful in all of Australia.

The Central Lowlands

Beyond the Great Dividing Range stretches the huge Central Lowlands. They span the entire continent from south to north. The greater part of the lowlands is called the Great

Artesian Basin. The Central Lowlands are a land of cattle and sheep ranches and wheat farms, for the most part.

The Western Plateau

Beyond the lowlands, going westward, we gradually ascend the Western Plateau. It consists of an elevated plain, from 1,300 to 2,000 feet (400 to 600 meters) above sea level, that is interrupted here and there by low, rocky mountain ranges and hill districts up to 5,000 feet (1,500 meters) in elevation. The Western Plateau covers about half of the continent and coincides largely with deserts. A land of ranches, mines, and Aboriginal reserves, the Western Plateau has few inhabitants.

One of the most spectacular interruptions in the plateau is Uluru, or Ayers Rock. This enormous sandstone feature is an unbroken mass of rock. Aborigines regard it as sacred.

Scattered through the Western Plateau are other low mountains and hill districts, including the Macdonnell Range, Arnhem Land, and the Kimberleys Region. But the dominant impressions are of flat elevated plains and enormous distances.

Western Coastal Plain

In many places the plateau reaches to the coasts of Australia, but several narrow coastal lowlands occur. The most notable of these lies along the western, or Indian Ocean, coast, below the Darling Escarpment. Actually this escarpment has been eroded into a belt of hills, marking the descent from the Western Plateau to the western coastal plain.

The beautiful city of Perth, the only sizable urban center in Western Australia, lies in these lowlands. Most of the remainder of the western coastal plain is fertile, productive agricultural land.

The Great Barrier Reef

Also best regarded as a landform feature is the amazing Great Barrier Reef. Paralleling the Pacific coast of Queensland

The Kata Tjuta (or the Olgas) is a sandstone rock cluster that stands above the Western Plateau near Uluru, in the Northern Territory. The Western Plateau, a land of ranches, mines, and Aboriginal reserves, has few residents.

for 1,250 miles (2,000 kilometers), this constitutes the world's largest coral reef. Tiny living sea creatures built the reef by attaching their bodies to the accumulated skeletons of their ancestors over millions of years. Most of the reef lies just below the surface of the ocean, but in places small islands have formed, trapping sand and allowing colonization by plants.

The brilliant colors of the coral and the fish living in the reef make it a major tourist attraction. Scuba divers and snorkelers come from all over the world to see the Great Barrier Reef.

In recent years, the reef has begun to experience severe damage. The main culprit seems to be warming of the ocean waters, which kills the algae upon which the living coral feed. Rising sea levels due to global warming present another problem.

UNIQUE FLORA AND FAUNA

Australia, like other continents, has not remained in one place. Instead, it broke away from Antarctica, Africa, and South America eons ago and drifted northeast. During most of this strange journey, the continent was isolated from all others.

Isolation allowed unique forms of plant and animal life to develop. Among the animals, marsupials became dominant. Marsupials are mammals that place the newborn offspring in maternal pouches for additional development. Marsupials existed before continental drift began, and in the Americas the opossum is an example.

In isolated Australia, the marsupials developed into many distinctive animals, such as kangaroos, wombats, and koalas. Other unique species also developed, such as the duck-billed platypus, an egg-laying, web-footed water creature.

Australia shares with Africa the crocodile, a danger to swimmers in many waterways. Another danger is the wide variety of Australian snakes—all of them deadly.

The continent also evolved its own versions of the giant flightless birds of southern Africa, represented in Australia by the emu. Another flightless bird, the dwarf penguin of Australia's southern coast, demonstrates the continent's former link to Antarctica. Phillip Island, near Melbourne, is the best place to see those endangered penguins.

When traveling in rural areas, drivers must be on the watch for kangaroos, one of Australia's many distinctive animals. Some Australians install "roo bars" on the front of their vehicles for protection.

Introduced Animals

Until about 50,000 years ago, no invader animal species except birds and fish reached Australia. Then Aborigines came, bringing dogs with them, and some of those canines evolved into the wild dingo, a meat-eating predator.

With the European colonization of Australia came many wild animals. The most destructive were the rabbit and the fox

DARLING DOWNS–MORETON
RABBIT BOARD
Rabbits not allowed in Qld
PENALTY $1000

G. Kennaugh
Clerk of the Board

This sign at a rabbit fence along the border between Queensland and New South Wales seems to presume that rabbits can read. The fence tries to stop the spread of rabbits, which were introduced to Australia by English settlers.

(introduced so the English could continue their pastime of fox hunting). Repeated attempts to eradicate the rabbit have proven futile. An enormous fence was erected across Australia to try to stop the spread of rabbits, but it has proven only partially successful.

Eucalyptus

One genus of trees, the *Eucalyptus*, dominates Australia. No other continent has so little variety in its forests. Australians call eucalyptus trees "gum" trees.

And yet the woodlands of Australia are far from uniform. The eucalyptus has adapted to almost every habitat on the continent. In wet areas, eucalyptus rain forests occur— multilayered and dense, often with ferns at ground level. In the deserts, in places where the subsurface water table is shallow, eucalyptus thrives, even in the Red Heart region. In semiarid regions, scrub forests of eucalyptus thrive. Only in the driest, rockiest places is the eucalyptus absent. One such region, Nullarbor, in the far south, consists of a vast grassland.

HUMAN IMPACT

The Aborigines had relatively little impact on Australia's natural vegetation. They did use fire to remove undergrowth and make hunting easier.

Europeans, by contrast, greatly diminished the Australian woodlands. To make pastures for enormous numbers of sheep and cattle, they cleared forest and planted introduced grasses. More forests fell to provide cultivated fields. Many native grasses suffered from overgrazing. Soil erosion resulted in some areas.

Other native forests have been replaced by commercial pine plantations. Pine trees from other continents grow in huge commercial forests for the lumber industry, part of Australia's effort to be more self-sufficient economically and to develop new export products.

The amount of environmental damage and change caused by Euro-Australians in just over two centuries far exceeds the changes wrought by Aborigines in 70,000 years.

CONCLUSION

The Australian habitat, then, can be described as largely flat in terrain, moisture-deficient in climate, half-tropical in latitude, exotic in native plant and animal life, and significantly modified by the human presence. All in all, one would not have expected one of the world's wealthiest countries to develop on this continent. In fact, for 50,000 years before the late eighteenth century, Australia's inhabitants had only a stone-age culture. To understand how modern Australia became an essentially happy, prosperous nation, it is vital to know more about its historical development.

From ancient times, Aborigines created artwork on the walls of caves, such as this example in the Kakadu National Park in the Northern Territory. Aboriginal art remains distinctive and highly accomplished today.

3

Australia Through Time

For millions of years, Australia drifted on its continental plate, completely uninhabited by humans or any other primates. And yet, in spite of the isolation, Australia received its first *Homo sapiens*—modern human beings—long before Europe or North America.

THE FIRST IMMIGRANTS

Modern humans first migrated out of Africa perhaps as long as 50,000 years ago. They reached Australia remarkably fast, passing along the southern coast of Arabia and Asia, then crossing a long-vanished land bridge into New Guinea. From there, they used stepping-stone islands to cross the Torres Strait and reach Cape York on the Australian continent, possibly as early as 50,000 years ago.

To judge from genetic evidence, the first group was joined over the next several thousand years by three or four other small bands. Collectively, they became the ancestors of the modern Australian Aborigines.

All Alone

Then, equally incredibly, no other human beings arrived in Australia for ages. The Aborigines remained all alone on their isolated continent for as much as 47,000 years.

In this long solitude, they spread out, adapting to the diverse habitats of Australia and its nearby islands. They split into some 500 tribes speaking 200 to 300 different but related languages. The best estimate of their numbers at the time of the first European colonization in 1788 is about 750,000.

The Prehistoric Continent

Aborigines had no writing system. This means that their enormously long period of isolation all belongs to Australian prehistory.

The continent entered written history only in 1616, when Dutch explorers became the first Europeans to arrive. For some three decades, the Dutch probed the shores of the continent, but made no settlements.

One Dutch ship wrecked on the west coast. Recent DNA genetic research confirmed that some of the Dutch sailors survived and mixed with the Aborigines on the western coast of Australia, leaving modern descendants.

Aboriginal Culture

Despite having no writing system and living at a Stone Age level, lacking any kind of metal-working, the Aborigines developed a rich and regionally varied culture. They lived as hunters, gatherers, and fishers. The boomerang is a hunting device they developed.

In their nature-based religion, a highly distinctive cosmology developed. For example, they believed that unless they regularly talked about the Earth, it would cease to exist. Aborigines did not believe in an afterlife.

From ancient times, they created wonderful artwork on the walls of caves that rivaled the more famous cave art of the ancient Cro-Magnon people of southwestern Europe in quality. In recent decades, similarly distinctive paintings by modern Aborigines have become much sought-after by collectors all over the world.

They also created music. A unique woodwind instrument, the didgeridoo, is an Aboriginal invention. During a ceremony in Sydney in 2002 commemorating the Australians who died in the Bali terrorist bombing, a dirge was played on the didgeridoo. The instrument has become part of Australian popular culture.

A Conquered People

No military match for the Europeans, the Aborigines suffered defeat and slaughter. Their numbers declined severely, and they disappeared altogether from Tasmania.

Their culture, too, declined as white Australians imposed their way of life on the Aborigines. In the most notorious episode, beginning in the 1950s, their children were taken from them to be educated in English-language boarding schools. The project was designed to force Euro-Australian culture upon them. Today, only 44,000 still speak a native language.

Recent decades have brought restoration of many land areas to the Aborigines. Their numbers have increased to about 430,000. Still, life is not easy for the Aborigines. They suffer from alcoholism, discrimination, poverty, poor health, and continued cultural decline. Among the most successful in retaining their culture have been the Torres Strait Islanders, who live on a group of small islands north of Cape York, the

Life today is not easy for Australia's Aborigines, the continent's original settlers. They have suffered from discrimination, poverty, poor health, and cultural decline.

northerneasternmost point on the continent. These Islanders, however, are more closely related to the people of New Guinea than to the Aborigines.

PRISON COLONY

Australia is at once an ancient, prehistoric land and a very new country. Alongside the almost unimaginably old native culture live the relatively newly arrived Euro-Australians.

In 1788, the United Kingdom established the first permanent European colony at Sydney. Australia was to be a penal colony, a place to dump convicted British felons and other criminals.

Between 1788 and the 1860s, when Great Britain stopped sending convicts, some 165,000 arrived in Australia. Most had committed only relatively minor offenses, such as stealing food when in need. Some were political prisoners, especially Irish freedom fighters.

Many of the convicts perished en route or soon after arrival in Australia. One book that deals with convict migration is *The Fatal Shore* by Robert Hughes. Today, most Aussies consider it an honor to be descended from the convicts in the first ships. These prisoners are called "First Fleeters," and their burial places, where known, have special honorific markers.

Almost from the first, free immigrants also came. Many were "assisted" settlers—poor people who required government subsidies to make the migration. Convicts and free settlers created new settlements on the small coastal plains, following the initial colony at Sydney. Tasmania was first settled in 1803; Western Australia at Albany in 1827 and at Perth in 1829; Victoria at Melbourne in 1835; South Australia at Adelaide in 1836; and Queensland at Brisbane in 1842. Those were initially all small, isolated footholds separate from one another.

Exploration

Meanwhile, exploration of the continent continued. Matthew Flinders became the first to circumnavigate Australia from 1801 to 1803, carefully mapping the entire coast. Two overland expeditions from 1860 to 1862 became the first to cross the continent from south to north, revealing for the first time the desert character of the Red Centre. Numerous other expeditions were undertaken, and the continent's physical geography at last became known.

The Frontier

A settlement frontier much like that in North America developed behind each of the separate early coastal settlements. Gradually some of those grew together and coalesced, except for Tasmania, separate because of its island status, and Western Australia, where deserts proved a barrier.

Just as in America, the frontier had gold rushes and outlaw bands (called bushrangers). A gold rush of 1851–1852 brought many people to Australia, including some from California. The most notorious bushrangers were the Kelly Gang. They became folk heroes of sorts—symbols of the convicts' struggle against British law and authority. The leader, Ned Kelly, was finally captured and executed in 1880, ending the era of the wild frontier.

Whether convict or free, assisted or unassisted, the European immigrants who created the coastal colonies and expanded the settlement frontier came mainly from the British Isles. By 1900, Great Britain and Ireland had sent about one million settlers to Australia.

The English

England dominated the early phase of migration. Some 92 percent of the convicts on the first four fleets of ships, between 1788 and 1792, came from England. Overall, 73 percent of all convicts were English.

In later decades, the English dominance faded. Still, they had a great shaping influence on Australia. For example, the English dialect spoken in Australia is "Cockney," derived from the speech of London's lower classes.

The numbers of English-born peaked in 1891 at 459,000. By the time of Australian independence in 1901, the English accounted for about 56 percent of the population from the British Isles. They formed the majority in every Australian state.

The Anglo-Australians came from two main areas of

IN
LOVING MEMORY
of
HENRY,
YOUNGEST SON OF
STEPHEN HART,
OF FULSCOT FARM, SOUTH MORETON,
BERKSHIRE, ENGLAND,
BORN JULY 21, 1856,
DIED AT BARDEEN, JULY 20, 1903.

A native of a shire near London is buried in Northam, Western Australia. English colonists, the most numerous British group that came to Australia, had great influence in shaping the country.

England. London and nearby shires of southeast England were one main source area. The other was in western and northern England. Cornwall, the westernmost part of England, ranked very high among English birthplaces. Wales, by contrast, sent very few settlers to Australia.

The Irish

Ireland provided the second largest immigrant group, coming both from what is today the independent Republic of Ireland (Eire) and from British-ruled Northern Ireland. At the time of the Australian immigration, all of Ireland belonged to the United Kingdom.

Although many Irish came as convicts, far greater numbers arrived as free settlers. The 1891 census of Australia counted 228,000 Irish-born, and they made up about 27 percent of the immigrants from the British Isles. The majority of them were Roman Catholics. Counties Tipperary, Limerick, and Clare—all in southern Ireland—sent the largest numbers.

Some say that Australia is the most Irish of all countries outside of Ireland. We perhaps find their imprint on Australia in the rough-and-ready, irreverent, and fun-loving qualities of the Aussies, not to mention their fondness for horse racing.

The Scots

Scots, who numbered 124,000 in 1891, account for about 14 percent of the British-derived population. Most were lowlanders, especially from the cities of Glasgow, Edinburgh, and Dundee.

But a very large contingent came from the rugged "highlands and islands" of northern Scotland. The highland shire of Inverness, including the west coast Isle of Skye, was a particularly notable source.

Many of the Scots immigrated to Australia after being evicted from their small tenant farms by landlords. The landowners wanted to create huge sheep ranches, and "clearances" to remove the tenants were part of that process.

BECOMING A NATION

In the long run, these immigrants created a prosperous nation. "Australia Fair," to use the words of the national anthem, became one of the world's "lucky" countries.

When Australia achieved independence in 1901, it was largely a nation of British immigrants. During the twentieth century, perhaps another two million British and Irish arrived. In 2000, 1.164 million of them were still living, forming 26 percent of Australia's foreign-born population.

Moreover, by 2000, natives of New Zealand—mainly of British descent, too—made up the second-largest foreign-born group, numbering 375,000. New Zealanders have the legal right to immigrate to Australia if they wish.

How did these diverse peoples become unified into a nation? Many factors, one of which was war, contributed.

Going To War

After independence, most Australians continued to think of themselves as British. When World War I came, Australia at once sided with the United Kingdom. Its troops saw action mainly against the Turkish Empire, an ally of Germany.

One battle against Turkey helped define a separate Australian identity. In the so-called Dardanelles Campaign, an effort was made to seize the narrow sea straits connecting the Mediterranean and Black Seas. An epic battle occurred near the small town of Gallipoli in 1915 and 1916, on the Dardanelles Strait. The Turks beat back this assault, inflicting incredibly high casualties on the Australian troops. This terrible defeat and enormous loss of lives helped bond Australians into one people, even more tightly than British origin could have done.

The terrorist attack at Kuta in Indonesia in 2002 killed a far disproportionate number of Aussies. The attack was Australia's own 9/11, and in a way, Kuta was a second Gallipoli, bonding Australians even as it inflicted grief.

Diversifying Immigration

After World War I, the sources of Australian immigrants began to diversify. A rigorously enforced "White Australia

Policy" meant that only Europeans were admitted, not Asians or Africans.

Some German settlers had arrived even in the nineteenth century, colonizing especially the Barossa Valley north of Adelaide in South Australia. But after 1920, another wave of non-British settlers came from Italy. The Italians went both to major cities and to rural areas, particularly interior New South Wales and coastal eastern Queensland.

World War II

Australia was on the front lines in World War II, facing the Japanese. Darwin, the capital of the Northern Territory, was severely damaged by Japanese bombs, and other northern towns also suffered air raids.

Australian troops fought most notably in Malaya, New Guinea, and Indonesia. They aided greatly in the defeat of Japan, defending their homeland in the most difficult of circumstances.

Recruiting More White Australians

The immigration of southern and southeastern Europeans increased greatly after World War II. Many more Italians came, joined by large contingents of Greeks, Serbs, and Croats. Serbs and Croats came from Yugoslavia, a country that no longer exists. Christian Arabs from Lebanon also immigrated in sizable numbers.

By 2000, Italy ranked fourth among Australia's foreign-born, the former Yugoslavia fifth, and Greece seventh. Germans formed the eighth-largest group.

Asian Immigration

Australia abandoned its "Europeans only" immigration policy in the early 1970s. Among the first to come after the repeal were Turks. Much larger numbers came from China, Vietnam, India, and Malaysia, though. By 2000, these nationalities ranked

A Serbian Orthodox Church at Wodonga in Victoria shows the new face of immigration to Australia in the twentieth century. Immigration by Italians, Greeks, Serbs, and Croats increased after World War II. In the early 1970s, Australia ended its "Europeans only" immigration policy, opening the country to Asians.

third, sixth, ninth, and tenth, respectively, among the foreign-born groups in Australia. From 1995 to 2000, Chinese made up more than 8 percent of all immigrants.

The Philippines has also been a significant source of immigrants. Perhaps most surprising is the low ranking of Indonesia, Australia's giant neighbor to the north, which has a population of about 230 million—more than ten times the number of Australians. The government of the continent-nation quite frankly fears mass, uncontrolled immigration from Indonesia and favors immigrants from other Asian countries. Five percent of Australia's total population today is of Asian birth or descent.

Becoming White Asians

Australia actively participated in the Korean and Vietnam wars. The Asian conflicts, Australians felt, directly threatened them.

These wars, however, coupled with World War II, served to convince the Australians that geographic location made them, in fact, Asians rather than Europeans. This realization, in turn, helped change their immigration policies and stimulated trade with Asian countries.

An Immigrant Country

The continued and diversified influx of foreigners has made Australia, far more than even the United States, a land of immigrants. About 25 percent of all Australians are foreign-born today, more than double the proportion in the United States, which is 11 percent.

Each year, at least 80,000 additional immigrants gain legal entry to Australia. They are carefully chosen on the basis of ethnic origin, skills, education, and wealth. An additional 12,000 refugees are admitted annually, carefully selected on their ability to integrate into Australian society.

Many British-descended Australians fear being over-whelmed by Asian immigrants. Some right-wing politicians have campaigned for office on anti-immigrant platforms, but with relatively little success.

Illegal Immigration

These fears of Asian domination have been heightened by a recent upsurge in illegal immigration. Small boats can easily reach the north coast of Australia from Indonesia.

On these boats are some Indonesians, but many more Middle Easterners. Indonesia is more of a conduit for illegal immigrants than a source of them.

As usual, Australians find humor in this situation. One

television comedian said, "Yes, we must halt the alien hordes coming from across the sea! (Pause) I mean, of course, New Zealanders!"

CONCLUSION

Ancient and modern. Aboriginal and European. Prehistoric covered with only a thin veneer of history. English, Irish, and Scottish, with a dash of Asian, Italian, Slavic, Greek, Turk, Arab, and New Zealand "Kiwis" thrown in for good measure. A small nation in numbers that went to war four times in the twentieth century and received diverse immigrants, becoming a distinctive, unique nation in the process. A country of immigrants on a continent inhabited for more than 50,000 years. Australia is all of this and more.

Darwin is a long way off, according to this distance marker on the Stuart Highway, which runs from Adelaide in the south to Darwin in the north. From this spot, it is about 81 miles to Alice Springs and about 1,006 miles to Darwin.

CHAPTER

4

Australia Is One?

O ur seventh major theme in the geographical study of Australia was posed as a question—"Australia: one or many?" Ask the typical Aussie and the answer will come back as a resounding "one!" The prevailing national idea, or perhaps more accurately, national myth, is that the diverse immigrants from the British Isles intermarried to become one people.

THE NATIONAL IDEA

The "Australia Is One" idea claims that the English, Irish, Scots, and smaller British groups rather quickly fused into a composite Anglo-Celtic culture. In fact, the term *Anglo-Celtic* is used widely in Australia.

The British and Irish populations generally did not form separate colonies or communities when they immigrated. Instead, the argument goes, they intermarried to form an "amalgam" or "alloy" unique to Australia, a mixture that never existed in the British Isles, where each group remained seated in its ancient homeland. The result in Australia was a "genetic and cultural average" of Anglo-Saxon (English) and Celtic (Irish, Scots, Cornish, and Welsh) components. Australians, then, see themselves as unique. Their ancestors melded together into a new people.

The belief is that the more diverse recent immigrants will also be drawn into this fused culture. Italians, Slavs, Greeks, Lebanese, and even Asians will eventually become ingredients in the mixture. Racial mixing with the Aborigines is already pretty well advanced. One example was a famous tennis star from several decades ago, Evonne Goolagong.

Cultural Uniformity?

It follows, then, that if Australians are one people, then no cultural differences of consequence exist from one region or state to another on the continent. Western Australians are like Queenslanders and Taswegians (as the people of Tasmania call themselves). In this view, Australia is different from the United States, where cultural sectional differences remain strong, distinguishing the South from the North, the West from the East, and the Midwest from New England. In contrast, a "white tribe of Asia" supposedly formed early in colonial Australia.

Mateship

The trigger mechanism that led to mixing, say the Aussies, was a bonding among the early convict immigrants. Their isolation, coupled with a common fate and suffering, led them to feel like a united group and quickly to discard being English, Irish, or Scottish.

The Australians even have a word for this "misery loves company" bonding. They call it *mateship*, a word still heard in modern Australia to explain and describe their national unity and oneness as a people. An attempt was even made to insert the word *mateship* into a revised constitution in 1999.

Crocodile Dundee

In their effort to create the image of "One Australia," Aussies have (as most nations do) resorted to a stereotype. They believe that the real Australia lies in the Bush, or even the Outback. Never mind that close to nine of every ten Australians live in cities. They share this rural myth with Texans and with the English, among others.

So, it is not surprising when a character such as "Crocodile" Dundee appears on your movie screen pretending to be the typical Aussie. Dundee's surname is Scottish, but his behavior is that of a rural frontiersman. Other books and movies, such as *The Thorn Birds, A Town Called Alice,* and *The Man from Snowy River*, similarly convey the image of a rural Australia.

Perhaps the most revealing statement of Australia's rural self-image is Aussie Dorothea Mackellar's enormously popular poem, "My Country." Its second stanza begins:

> *I love a sunburnt country,/A land of sweeping plains,*
> *Of ragged mountain ranges,/Of droughts and flooding rains.*

Although the idea of rural Australia is persistent, urban Australia does get some attention, too. The classic comedy film *Muriel's Wedding,* starring Toni Collette, for example, focuses on the lives of urban Australians. Still, the prevailing national stereotype is a rough-and-ready, beer-swilling, crocodile-fighting, resourceful, fearless man of the Bush—which is, of course, far from the truth.

ANGLO-CELTIC CULTURE

A lot of evidence suggests that the concepts of "Australia Is One" and "Anglo-Celtic culture" have some validity. Language provides one example. An Australian dialect of English exists. The differences in speech from one region and state to another are far weaker than in the United States. Vocabulary and pronunciation are fairly uniform.

If you look hard enough, you can find some words that are unique to one region or another. For example, Taswegians use the word *tier* to mean "mountain ridge." It requires a serious search to find such words, though. For all practical purposes, one national dialect exists, and it is essentially a variant of the Cockney dialect of the lower classes of London. In Australia, residents do not speak with an Irish brogue or the lilt of a Scottish accent. Everyone, regardless of where their ancestors came from in the British Isles, speaks the nasal, twangy, modified Cockney English.

First Effective Settlement

What gave Cockney the upper hand? The concept called "first effective settlement" helps explain what happened.

The idea of "first effective settlement" holds that the first group of immigrant settlers to establish a viable colony on a new continent exerts the largest influence in shaping the culture. This is true even if larger numbers of people from a different place arrive later.

The first effective colonization of Australia was achieved by transported criminals mainly from the London area—in other words, members of the lower class who spoke the Cockney dialect. Their speech still prevails today.

Place Names

Anglo-Celtic culture is more complicated than that, however. Australia is more than just a transplanted piece of London. It is truly a blending.

The place names of Australia offer evidence of this mixture. For example, a town named for one in England often lies next to one named for an Irish or Scottish place, and those names almost never mean that the people of the town descend mainly from one British group.

Maclean, in northeastern New South Wales, bills itself as "the Scottish town in Australia." True, its name is Scottish, and

In southeastern Queensland, Killarney, named for an Irish town, is near Warwick, named for an English town. Strangely, Warwick has a large number of people of Irish descent and Killarney has few. Such oddities abound in Australia and show how Anglo-Celtic culture has blended.

a lot of people with Scottish ancestors live there. Trace the birthplaces on epitaphs in the local cemetery, however, and it will be clear that more natives of England than Scotland lived there. The "Scottish town" is actually in the tourism business and pretends to be more Scottish than it really is.

Scottish Names on the Land

Another example of "misleading" place names comes from eastern Australia. There, many towns, villages, and "stations" (as ranches are called in Australia) bear the Scottish word elements *glen* (valley), *strath* (elongated valley), and *inver* (river mouth). Many other places in this region bear the names of Scottish shires, such as Ayr.

One might easily come to the conclusion that the greater part of the Eastern Highlands was settled by Scots. That is not the case, though. Virtually everywhere in this swath of Scottish place names, English and Irish settlers outnumbered the Scots.

The answer to this puzzle reveals something about Australian Anglo-Celtic culture. Scottish names such as "Glen Ellen" or "Strathmore" were perceived as pretty and romantic. Also, the literary works of Sir Walter Scott about romantic, rural Scotland were very popular when most of those places were named. Australians of all ancestries used Scottish names simply because they liked them. The names became part of a composite culture.

RELIGIOUS DENOMINATIONS

In the British Isles, religious affiliation had a strong ethnic meaning. Most English were Anglicans, Scots were Presbyterians, the great majority of Irish were Roman Catholic, and the Cornish and Welsh were Methodists.

In this respect, Australia did not become one. The major British immigrant denominations survived. Today there are nearly 5 million Catholics, 4 million Anglicans, and 676,000 Presbyterians. Although the Methodists and several other Protestant denominations submerged their identities in the 1.35 million-member Uniting Church, most of the old denominational lines held fast.

Moreover, the large Greek and Serbian immigrations built an Eastern Orthodox Christian Church of 500,000, and Germans remained true to a 250,000-member Lutheran Church. Add to this mix some 201,000 Muslims, and Australia emerges as a multidenominational country.

Still, even in this diversity, a sense of oneness can be detected. The country has no dominantly Catholic, Protestant, or Muslim regions. Nothing comparable exists to, say, the Catholic zone in Hispanic and French Louisiana areas in the southern United States.

In addition, an "Australia Is One" idea is perhaps implied by the roughly 5 million people who report no religious faith—about one-fourth of the population. Some describe Australia as a "post-Christian" society, though that is certainly an exaggeration. Many Aussies are devout Christians.

GOVERNMENT

Most powerfully, the national government helps build the concept of "Australia Is One." The first theme of the book, "the continent-nation," describes this potent and enduring force of unity.

Australia, the sixth-largest country in the world in terms of land area, is governed as a democracy and achieved both its union and independence in 1901. Before that, Australia consisted of a series of separate British colonies, like the United States before 1776.

The Australian democracy is based on that of the United Kingdom. The government has an elected Parliament and prime minister. A Cabinet is appointed to deal with the various branches of the government. The level of personal freedom is remarkably high. In freedom of the press, Australia ranks as the twelfth best country in the world (Canada is the fifth and the United States the seventeenth).

The seat of government is in Canberra, in the Australian Capital Territory. Beautifully situated in the Great Dividing Range, Canberra was created early in the twentieth century as a new capital city, just as Washington, D.C., was built in the eighteenth century for the United States. It became the capital in 1927. Canberra, like Washington, has wide boulevards and graceful circles. It sits beside artificial Lake Burley Griffin, named for the American who designed the city. At the center of Canberra, atop Capitol Hill, stands the futuristic Parliament House. Greater Canberra has a population of almost 350,000.

The Australian government is federal. That is, power is shared with the six states and, to a lesser extent, with the two

The futuristic Parliament House stands atop Capital Hill in Canberra, the seat of Australia's democratic government. Canberra was constructed in the early twentieth century to be the capital city.

territories. In this sense, Australia resembles the United States, which also has a federal government.

All citizens 18 and older are required to vote. They can be fined $50 (Australian) for not showing up at the voting polls.

THE MONARCHY

Though fully independent, Australia, like Canada, retains ties to the British Empire and to its royal family. Queen Elizabeth II is represented in Australia by a governor general, whose role is essentially ceremonial.

Many Australians want to sever ties with Great Britain and become a republic. In 1999, a referendum was held on the issue. A clear majority favored keeping the monarchy.

This vote also revealed some evidence in favor of the "Australia Is One" concept, or at least of the notion of an Anglo-Celtic culture. The majority favoring the monarchy was not large, but most of the descendants of the English, Scottish, and even Irish Catholic settlers—the Anglo-Celtic population—voted strongly in favor of the monarchy.

The referendum also brought out the Aussies' irreverent sense of humor. The prime minister at the time was John Howard, affectionately (or perhaps not so affectionately) called "Tubby." He favored keeping the monarchy. This prompted a headline in one of the country's leading newspapers: "Tubby Goes in to Bat for the Queen." Such informality and humor in the press reflects the deep-seated, classless sense of equality that lies at the root of Australian society.

POLITICAL PARTIES

Like the United States, Australia has political parties, three of which play dominant roles. One is the Australian Labor Party, with a center-left ideology similar to that of the Democratic Party in America. The other two, the Liberal Party and the National Party, have formed a center-right coalition that is similar to the American Republican Party.

Other splinter parties come and go, often supporting extreme views on such matters as Asian immigration. They remain minor players, though. Most Australians are centrists when it comes to politics. That contributes still more support for "Australia Is One."

STANDARD OF LIVING

Australia is a wealthy country. Its roughly 20 million people enjoy one of the highest standards of living in the world. This, too, helps foster "Australia Is One."

Perhaps the best measure of living standards is the infant mortality rate—the number of babies per 1,000 live births who die before their first birthday. The rate is a good index because it reflects nutrition, health care, and education. Australia's infant mortality rate is 5.2, lower even than the United States's rate of 6.6. For the entire world, the rate is 54.0.

In earlier times, many children died in Australia. As this headstone shows, a rural family from Yorkshire in England lost three children in a little over four years in the 1860s. Today, however, Australia's infant mortality rate is lower than that of the United States.

Australia was not always blessed with such a low infant mortality rate. In the nineteenth century, alarming numbers of children died. Independent Australia steadily built a superb medical care system, however, which reduced death rates for infants, children, and adults alike. Even Aussies who live in remote places enjoy access to medical care from the Royal Flying Doctor Service. These doctors make house calls by small airplane.

The Royal Flying Doctor Service provides medical care to remote areas, using small aircraft and dirt landing strips. This unit is based at Mount Isa in western Queensland.

Nearly all well-to-do countries also have small families. The total fertility rate, or TFR, is the number of children the average woman bears during her lifetime. To produce "zero population growth," a TFR of 2.1 is required. Australia's TFR, which in 1901 stood at 3.93, dropped below the zero growth rate by 1981, when the TFR was 1.94. Today, it stands at 1.7. The average world rate is 2.8.

Now, the total fertility rate has to remain at or below 2.1 for some decades before the natural increase of the population ceases. Australia has not yet reached that point. Its rate of natural population change stands above 0.6 percent per year. That means births still exceed deaths.

Part of the reason for the continued natural increase in population is that Australians have good medical care, which allows them to live long lives. The average life expectancy is 82 years for women and 76 for men, with an overall average of 80 years. The United States, by comparison, has an average life expectancy of 77 years for the total population.

Income provides another measure of wealth. The average purchasing power per person amounts to $25,000 (American dollars), far higher than the world average of $7,150.

Pockets of Poverty

Still, not all Aussies are doing that well. Earlier, the generally bad plight of the Aborigines was mentioned. A recent government study concluded that some 2 million Australians lived in poverty. Many such people live in isolated pockets on the outer fringes of towns and cities. The majority of those impoverished people were not Aborigines.

One Serbian-Australian taxi driver complained about making so little money. "Australia is a wonderful country if you have money," he declared. "Too bad I don't!"

A growing divide between rich and poor was noted as early as 1991. That divide now threatens, in the words of one newspaper editorial, to become "a yawning chasm."

It's No Paradise

So, Australia is no paradise. Recent government studies revealed additional social problems. They found that many Aussies have gambling problems or are addicted to drugs and alcohol. Rates of personal assault, rape, and burglary are also rising rapidly, and the youth suicide rate stands among the highest in the world.

TOO MANY AUSTRALIANS?

These problems suggest that Australia has many people for whom it cannot provide jobs and services. A recent book by Erik Paul asks the question: *Australia: Too Many People?*

Certainly, the population of the country has grown rapidly.

In 1901, at the time of independence, the number of inhabitants stood at 3,800,000. This grew to 10.3 million by 1960, and the total has almost doubled since then. Immigration has become the leading cause of the population increase.

The issue, then, is whether Australia should place stricter limits on immigration. If it does not, some people express concerns that Australia may not possess the resources to absorb additional large numbers of people without lowering living standards.

Some point to the fact that most of Australia remains essentially empty. Over one-third of all Aussies live in New South Wales, another quarter in Victoria, and 19 percent in Queensland. That adds up to 78 percent, nearly all of whom live in the eastern coastal Green Crescent part of those states. Moreover, with each passing decade, the Australian interior loses population. People are migrating out of the Red Heart, making it even emptier. This situation begs the question: Why not send millions of new immigrants into the interior? The answer is that the desert's "red heart, dead heart" simply cannot support them.

Absorbing Non-British Immigrants

The other burning issue concerning immigration is whether the idea of "Australia Is One" can endure ongoing non-British immigration. Can mateship and the Anglo-Celtic culture be made to accommodate Asian immigrants?

Can Turks or Chinese or Malaysians be drawn into one community? A recent census found that 2.5 million Australians spoke a language other than English at home. It also found, though, that the large majority of these people also know English. Immigrant bilingualism is the rule rather than the exception and intermarriage rates remain high. Given these facts, maybe the national idea can survive.

A rancher herds his livestock at a cattle station in the Outback. Most land use in Australia is for livestock ranching. Australia produces 16 percent of the world's exported beef.

CHAPTER

5

Making a Living

Australians make their living in various ways, and those occupations differ from one region to another. Economically, at that level, "Australia Is One" does not exist. True, most Aussies live in large cities and find employment in industries of different sorts. Rural and small-town Bush Australia, however, is a vivid patchwork of diverse enterprises.

PRIMARY INDUSTRIES

Most Outback and Bush enterprises are involved in primary industries, which extract raw materials or produce unprocessed goods. Examples include mining, agriculture, fishing, and lumbering. The hunting and gathering pursued by some Aborigines also constitute primary industries.

Agriculture

Australia is not richly endowed with good farmland. Just 6 percent of its land area is cropland. Another 55 percent can be used as pasture. Today, only about 4 percent of the work force finds employment in agriculture. The red heart, dead heart is not the "fruited plain" enjoyed by America. Most agriculture takes place in and on the fringes of the Green Crescent.

The major agricultural products, ranked in order of market value, are beef cattle, wheat, milk, wool, vegetables, fruits and nuts, grapes and wine, and mutton and lamb meat. If ranked by acreage, the leading crops are wheat, soybeans, canola oil (for cooking), grain sorghums, oats, hay, cotton, and sugarcane.

About 145,000 farms and ranches, employing 400,000 people, exist in the entire country. They produce only 4 percent of the gross domestic product (GDP)—the value of all goods and services produced in Australia. As recently as the 1950s, agricultural products provided almost 80 percent of Australia's exports. Its economy was a classic "agro-export" colonial type.

Today, that has changed. Agricultural exports are only one-third as valuable as the products of the mines and have only one-seventh the value of manufactured goods.

Agricultural Regions

The geography of types of agriculture reveals vivid differences from one region to another. One type is tropical cash-crop farming, found along the northeast coast in pockets of coastal plains. The main crops raised in this system are sugarcane, bananas, cotton, and pineapples. Australia takes full agricultural advantage of its location, which is half in the tropics.

A second type of agriculture is market gardening,

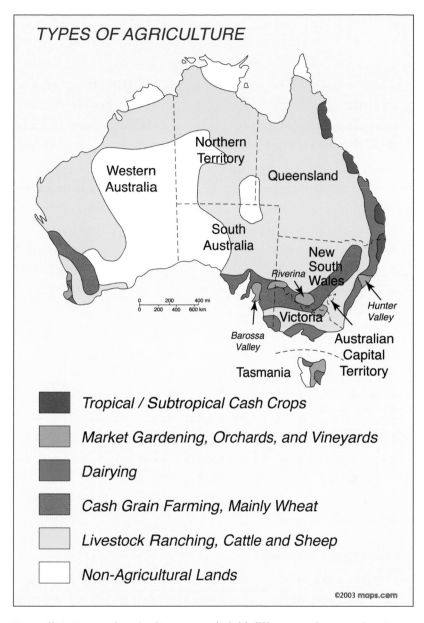

TYPES OF AGRICULTURE

Northern Territory

Western Australia

Queensland

South Australia

New South Wales

Riverina

Hunter Valley

Barossa Valley

Victoria

Australian Capital Territory

Tasmania

0   200   400 mi
0   200   400   600 km

Tropical / Subtropical Cash Crops

Market Gardening, Orchards, and Vineyards

Dairying

Cash Grain Farming, Mainly Wheat

Livestock Ranching, Cattle and Sheep

Non-Agricultural Lands

©2003 maps.com

Australia's types of agriculture reveal vivid differences from region to region. Cash crops, market gardening, and dairying involve intensive use of the land, with a large input of labor and capital investment and a high output per unit of land. Cash grain farming and livestock ranching represent extensive use of the land, in which huge tracts of marginal land are required to be viable.

orchards, and vineyards. This involves the raising of mid-latitude cash crops such as vegetables, citrus fruit, apples, pears, macadamia nuts, and grapes for wine and raisins. These areas, too, lie largely in small patches of coastal and interior plains. Notable among them are the Hunter and Barossa valleys, famous for wine, and the Riverina district in the Murray-Darling river basin. Tasmania is famous for apples, among other such produce.

Immigrants brought a northwestern European taste for cows' milk, butter, and cheese with them from the British Isles. Dairying developed early to supply these milk products. In time, certain districts rose to dominance in commercial dairying. These all lie in the Green Crescent region and have lush pastures.

Cash Grain Farming

Another type of agriculture is cash grain farming. Australia has two huge wheat belts, one in the west and the other in the south. These grain-growing areas lie in the transition zones between the humid and semiarid parts of Australia. Geographer Donald Meinig used the phrase "on the margins of the good earth" to describe the location of the wheat belts. This should not be surprising. In North America, too, a wheat belt characterizes much of the semi-arid Great Plains.

Livestock Ranching

Most land use in Australia is for livestock ranching, which is done both in the Outback and in the mountains of the Great Dividing Range. Sheep are more important in the southern, mid-latitude ranching areas, whereas beef cattle dominate the north. In recent decades, the cattle area has expanded southward as many ranchers shifted from sheep to cattle.

Even so, sheep remain far more numerous. Australia has

11.5 percent of all the sheep in the world, and produces one-third of the world's wool. It provides 27 percent of all wool entering the world foreign-trade market. Sheep outnumber people seven to one. At the same time, Australia produces 16 percent of the world's exported beef and huge amounts of mutton and lamb. Wool, beef, mutton, and lamb combined represent by far the largest component of Australia's agricultural output by cash value.

Ranching Aussie-Style

The American West has many cattle and sheep ranches just like Australia does. Ranching Aussie-style is a bit different, though.

For one thing, Australians use an entirely different vocabulary. A ranch is a "station," a pasture is a "paddock," a roundup is a "muster," a cattle drive is "overlanding," and so on. Australian livestock stations are on the average larger than American ranches.

Even the methods of handling range cattle are different. Instead of throwing a lasso, Australian ranchers crack a whip and are assisted by skilled herder dogs. Also, Australians still often drive cattle on hoof over trails to market, following officially established public "stock routes."

Mining

The Australian continent possesses significant amounts of minerals and metals. Mining plays a role in maintaining the country's position among the world's wealthy nations, although less than one percent of the labor force works in the mines.

The mineral wealth occurs in deposits scattered mainly through the Outback and shallow offshore waters. Aboriginal lands contain a large part of these resources.

Australia is the world leader in bauxite production. Aluminum is made from bauxite (though not in Australia).

A "stock route," or cattle trail, stretches across the state of Victoria in the far western part of the nation. Australians still often drive cattle on hoof to market along officially established trails.

Nearly 38 percent of the world's bauxite is produced here. The main deposits are at Weipa in far northern Queensland and at Gove in Arnhem Land, Northern Territory.

The country ranks second in the world in iron ore mining. Its iron ore is of the highest quality. The major iron mines are in Western Australia, at remote Pilbara, Newman, and Big Bell. The Port Pirie region of South Australia also has iron deposits.

Uranium, crucial in the atomic age, is also produced. Arnhem Land has the largest mines, especially at Coronation Hill. The biggest deposits are on Aboriginal land.

Australia ranks number two in the world in lead and zinc production. The main centers are Mount Isa in Queensland and Broken Hill and Cobar in the New South Wales Bush.

Oil, Natural Gas, and Coal

Australia also has petroleum and natural gas. The largest fields lie offshore, off the northern coast of Western Australia. In addition, the Flounder-Kingfish field is found off the Victoria coast. On the mainland, the only major oil and gas deposits are in South Australia's Outback.

Coal is mined in Queensland's Bowen Basin, in the Hunter Valley near Newcastle, and at Collie in western Australia. Australia also produces significant amounts of tin, manganese, gold, silver, copper, nickel, diamonds, opals, and sapphires. As with other mineral deposits, most of these are scattered in remote areas.

Mineral Exports

As recently as 1991, mines produced 42 percent of Australia's exports, by value. That declined to 29 percent by 2001, but minerals remain vitally important to the national economy.

Prices for minerals are volatile, going through pronounced ups and downs. For example, in the fiscal year ending June 30, 2002, B.H.P. Billiton—the largest mining company in Australia and the world—experienced a 12 percent decline in profits. Even so, the firm's annual profit was $1.93 billion (American dollars).

Most of the products of Australia's mining industry enter the export market. Japan is a major customer. The heavy reliance on mining, which replaced the earlier dependence on agricultural exports, meant that Australia has retained a "colonial" economy. That is, the country exports mainly the products of primary industries and imports manufactured goods.

Fishing and Forestry

Adding somewhat to the colonial character of the economy are fishing and timber exports. Neither has very much importance. Australia's bordering seas are not among the world's better fishing grounds.

The native eucalyptus forests did not yield much in the way of exports, either. Only where commercial forest plantations of exotic tree species replaced the native vegetation did a timber industry develop. Australia is now self-sufficient in timber production.

Major progress has recently been made in changing the character of Australia's economy. It has become less colonial in character. Much of this progress has occurred in the development of secondary industries.

SECONDARY INDUSTRIES

Manufacturing, also called secondary industry, was traditionally rare in Australia. Even today, Aussies joke about how few things they manufacture.

The process of manufacturing involves converting raw materials into finished products. About one of every five people in the Australian labor force works in manufacturing (including the construction industry).

Australia made a big push to increase manufacturing in the 1960s and succeeded. By 1981, more than one million people were employed and manufactured items accounted for 18 percent of the GDP. The value of manufactured goods exported is today more than twice that of minerals and metals.

The industries are very diverse and often produce luxury goods. For example, food processing is a major industry today, producing fine wines, famous beers such as Foster's, and good cheeses. Other major industries include machinery, diverse equipment, other metal products, metal processing, oil refining, lumber, meat, paper, cement, and printing and publishing. Newspaper and book publishing magnate Rupert Murdoch is Australian.

Manufacturing is concentrated in a relatively few locations. Nearly all factories are in port cities. This uneven development challenges the notion of "Australia Is One." Instead, Australia, in the manufacturing sense, is a series of coastal centers of industrial development serving huge rural interior hinterlands.

Buy Australian

One major factor encouraging Australian manufacturing is the country's policy to try to become less dependent upon imported goods. The term "import substitution" is sometimes used.

No better example can be found than a box of "Uncle Toby's Toasted Muesli" breakfast cereal. On each box is printed the following statement:

> This product is made in Australia. And just as importantly, the company that made it is Australian owned. When you buy products that are Australian made and owned, the money you spend stays right here in Australia.

Deindustrialization

In spite of all those efforts, manufacturing began a relative decline in Australia in the 1980s. Nearly every wealthy industrial country in the world underwent a similar decline. Australia was not unusual in this sense. The process is called deindustrialization.

As a result, employment in manufacturing declined to 933,000 by 2001. The contribution of manufactured goods to the GDP plummeted to only 12 percent.

SERVICE INDUSTRIES

The decline in manufacturing has been more than made up by growth in the service industries. These are sometimes referred to as tertiary industry. Service industries dominate the economy of most wealthy nations today, and Australia is no exception. Three-quarters of the country's work force finds employment in service industries.

Service industries neither extract resources nor manufacture goods. Instead, they include a broad range of activities such as government, education, health care, transportation, entertainment, energy production, legal services, finance, retailing, consulting, wholesaling, tourism, and so on.

The largest single service industry is retailing, which employs 15 percent of the work force. Australia might be described as a nation of shopkeepers. But the service industries are very diverse. One that deserves special attention is tourism.

Tourism

A long and vigorous advertising campaign finally began drawing substantial numbers of tourists in the 1980s. One pivotal event was the widely publicized bicentennial of the first European settlement of the country, celebrated in 1988.

The number of foreign tourists continued to soar after that. In 1991, 2.5 million arrived, and by 1999, the total reached 4.65 million. The Sydney Olympic Games of 2000 provided another big boost.

The leading countries of origin of foreign tourists are New Zealand (17 percent), Japan (15 percent), the United Kingdom (12 percent), and the United States (9 percent). The last few years have seen a decline, due to terrorism and the world economic situation. Still, tourism remains one of Australia's most important service industries and has become the fourth-largest sector of the "export" economy.

Foreigners come mainly to see the natural beauty of

Australia, in places such as Kakadu National Park in Arnhem Land, Uluru, the Great Barrier Reef, the Daintree Rain Forest of tropical Queensland, the deserts of the Outback, and the wonderful Pacific beaches of Queensland. They are also attracted by the beautiful and cosmopolitan cities, especially Sydney and Melbourne. Some venture out into the appealing rural countryside of the Green Crescent, including the wine districts.

Domestic tourism should not be overlooked, though. Australians love nothing more than going on vacation, and they often return year after year to the same place. In 2000, there were many millions of domestic tourist nights—the total number of nights spent away from home, in a hotel or motel. Campers are not included. Together, foreign and domestic tourists accounted for 4.5 percent of Australia's GDP.

Transportation

Australia's system of highways, railroads, and airlines—another service industry—is well developed, although the road and rail network does not extend into most parts of the desert Outback. Many roads also remain unpaved in sparsely settled areas.

As yet, the system of controlled-access interstate highways is not completely developed. The interstate that runs from Sydney to Canberra to Melbourne, called the "dual carriageway," is only now nearing completion. The cities of Brisbane, Adelaide, and Perth—each of which has more than a million inhabitants—remain unconnected to a national system of highways. Driving coast-to-coast is a real adventure that requires careful planning. Despite these difficulties, Aussies are automobile people. The country has about one car for every two people.

Railroads and Airlines

A transcontinental railroad also exists. One of the truly epic passenger train rides in the world is the "Indian-Pacific," which

The Indian-Pacific passenger train makes a brief stop in the Nullarbor region of Western Australia. The train runs 2,704 miles (4,352 kilometers) from Sydney to Perth and is named for the two oceans it connects.

runs 2,704 miles (4,352 kilometers), from Sydney to Perth. It is named for the two oceans it connects.

For long distances, airlines are the best way to travel. Even some relatively small Outback destinations are served by airlines. Australia has one dominant airline, Qantas, which also reaches many overseas destinations.

CONCLUSION

Australia's economy reveals rather vivid geography. One region is not like another. In one place is a valley filled with winemakers, in another a plain devoted to beef cattle ranching, in yet another there might be a mining town or a huge city dominated by service industries. A curious geographic pattern of mines, industrial cities, and areas of different types of agriculture exists.

Today, to a certain degree, every sizable country exhibits geographical patterns like that. Few of those other countries claim to be "One," though, as Australia does.

Sydney, the capital of the state of New South Wales, is also the country's largest city and made a name for itself on the world stage as the host of the 2000 Olympic Games.

6

Several Australias

Although some may believe that there are cracks in the façade of the "Australia Is One" concept, it certainly will not be proven by trying to find a country sharply divided into clear-cut regions. The contrasts within the nation are not of the same magnitude of America's fading sectionalism.

Instead, Australia is indeed a country in which regional differences play a minor role, although such differences *do* exist in subtle forms. Despite what the Australians may say, it is misleading to think of the country as "one." Perhaps "several Australias" is a better term to use.

CONTRAST AMONG THE STATES

Aussies will often admit that differences exist among the six states. Tasmania, they say, is the "most English" state and the most conservative, sheltered as it is on its island. It is, for example, the only state to make homosexuality a crime (though these laws are rarely enforced). An analysis of birthplaces listed on tombstones in Tasmania confirmed that, indeed, the largest element in the island's population had been Anglo-Saxons from the lowlands of England.

The other state most often described as distinctive is Western Australia. The state tourist bureau says simply that "the west is different." It does not say how. The densely populated part of Western Australia is in the far southwestern corner of this enormous state. Ringed by deserts, it is isolated in a way not unlike Tasmania's. Moreover, it shares with Tasmania a domination by lowland English settlers.

Queensland, because it was settled somewhat later, supposedly has a more amalgamated Australian character. Victoria, the "Garden State," has a demonstrably stronger Scottish flavor. The Northern Territory, in the popular mind, retains much of the character of the frontier—even if the once dusty and genuine town of Alice Springs, in the southern part of the territory, is today dominated by expensive boutiques.

There is another fundamental contrast among the states. New South Wales is home to 34 percent of the country's population. Victoria, in spite of its small geographical size, houses another 25 percent. Almost three-fifths of all Aussies, then, live in these two states alone.

Vernacular Regions

Popular perception of regionalism can also be observed on a scale smaller than states. Vernacular regions are those perceived to exist by the inhabitants of an area. These regions generally have accepted names or nicknames.

Every state and territory in Australia has many vernacular regions. Examples include New England, the name people give to interior northeastern New South Wales; Gippsland, as the eastern part of Victoria is called; and the Green Triangle, the southeasternmost corner of South Australia. Literally hundreds of these vernacular regions can be found.

It is hard to say what these mean in terms of regionalism. Just having a name does not necessarily mean that a region also has distinctive cultural qualities. Often, names reflect nothing more than characteristics of terrain, vegetation, or climate, as in the case of the Green Triangle. New England's population turns out, according to the epitaphs of the immigrant generation, to be a stronghold of highland Celts. It is as inappropriately named as New South Wales itself.

The division of Australia into vernacular regions, then, seems to be nothing more than a convenient device to cope with so large a country. People have a need to identify with a region, but it does not follow that cultural differences are the reason.

CITY LIFE

Eighty-five percent of all Australians live in urban areas. Just the five largest state capitals (excluding Hobart in Tasmania) plus Canberra, the national capital, account for more than 61 percent of the country's population.

Australian city life is distinctive. The major urban areas are cosmopolitan, clean, modern, comparatively very safe from crime, served by first-rate mass-transit systems, not dissected by expressways, and filled with imaginatively designed buildings. They are pedestrian-friendly and have abundant parks. Almost everyone who visits Australia finds its cities among the most livable in the world.

Central city blight and decay is virtually unknown. Downtowns remain vibrant, filled with shops, theaters, and museums. Sydney and Perth enjoy beautiful bayside locations and have fine ocean beaches.

Each major city has its own distinctive character, adding an element of regionalism to the urban scene. Sydney takes pride in its convict origins, its status as the largest Australian city, and

Part of the urban scene in Sydney includes row houses near the city's center. Each major city in Australia has its own distinctive character.

its stunningly beautiful harbor, next to which stands the world famous opera theater. Row houses near the city center add another touch of distinctiveness. The success of the 2000 Olympic Games is a source of great pride for the citizens of this world-class city.

Melbourne shares most of Sydney's virtues. Its people like to pretend that their ancestors included fewer transported felons, and they shamelessly put on the airs of the English upper class. That aside, Melbourne is a truly beautiful city with amenities that overwhelm even Americans.

Adelaide, another beautiful city, also denies that it has a convict heritage and styles itself the "city of churches." Never mind that few people attend these churches and that one of them has been converted into "St. Paul's Night Club." The central part of Adelaide is completely ringed by a broad belt of parks.

Even distant and isolated Perth is a beautiful and accommodating city, with every amenity imaginable. Greater Perth includes the seaside city of Fremantle.

To see major variations in the Australian urban scene, one should go to Canberra, a relatively new and somewhat sterile planned city with broad ceremonial boulevards. Like many national capitals, Canberra is designed to overwhelm the individual with the power and grandeur of the state.

The string of contiguous beachfront cities in far southeastern Queensland, south of Brisbane, is collectively called Gold Coast. Its population, some 405,000, exceeds that of Greater Canberra. Gold Coast looks much like south Florida—a chain of beachside hotels, condominiums, and expensive homes, behind which lie strips of shops and neighborhoods of middle-class housing. Gold Coast strikes the visitor as new, brash, sprawled, and unplanned.

City People

Not only is urban life distinctive as one of the Australian lifestyles, but the residents' origins are different from those of the people who live in the Bush and Outback. First, the great majority of the Asian and other non-British immigrants of the post-1970 period settled in the cities.

Earlier than that, the most common origin for the people who settled Australia's cities was the large cities of England, Scotland, and Ireland. Researchers learned this from reading the epitaphs on tombstones of the earlier immigrants. The founder of Melbourne was a native Londoner. Urban Britain was transplanted to urban Australia.

Aussie city dwellers differ in many ways from rural folk, too. This was most recently demonstrated in the national referendum on getting rid of the monarchy and making Australia a republic. The only areas that voted for the measure were the large cities—Sydney, Melbourne, Brisbane, Canberra, Adelaide, and Hobart.

Australia's cities, then, are both collectively distinctive and exhibit individual personalities. They suggest very strongly that Australia is several rather than one.

The Australian bush has two regional subdivisions, a lowland-plain crop and dairy region and a "Celtic" highland ranching area, as seen here in the Great Dividing Range of east-central New South Wales.

BUSH LIFE

The Bush can be defined as the rural areas and small towns lying within the Green Crescent area of Australia. Life there is very different from that in the cities.

These differences go back in large part to the period of settlement. The immigrants' epitaphs reveal that the large majority of Bush settlers came from the rural shires and counties of Great Britain and Ireland.

The Bush areas should be divided into two subregions: the pockets of coastal plain and the hilly and mountainous districts. In the coastal plain, whether along the Pacific coast in areas such as the Hunter Valley or on the Indian Ocean coast of Western Australia, intensive lowland types of agriculture prevail. Rural people from the lowlands of England and Scotland dominated the settlement of these fertile and productive plains.

Highland Stock Raisers

Beyond, especially in the hills and mountains of the Great Dividing Range, but also throughout the livestock ranching areas, highland people were the original settlers. Many came from the rugged highlands and islands of Scotland; the hilly shires and counties of western and northern England, especially Cornwall; and interior southern Ireland. They were, in effect, Celts.

The Celts had long raised range cattle and sheep in the British and Irish highlands. In Australia, they created a new pastoral hinterland and perpetuated many of their traditional herding ways.

The Australian Bush, then, has two major regional sub-divisions—a lowland-plain crop and dairy area and a highland ranching area. Once again, several Australias can be detected rather than one.

Often these regional differences can be seen in the rural dwellings of the Bush folk. For example, a "sawtooth"-roofed cottage derived from Cornwall appears widely through the "Celtic" part of the Bush, while a "Queensland raised cottage" standing above the ground on piers prevails in the northeast.

Certain other elements work to unify the Bush. Politically, the area is conservative and pro-monarchy, in contrast to the left-leaning cities that favor dumping the monarchy.

A "sawtooth"-roofed cottage derived from Cornwall, England, sits in Murrurundi in New South Wales. The cottage reflects the Celtic character of the Bush in the Great Dividing Range.

Also, throughout the Bush are scores of delightful small towns. These almost invariably have a cluster of fine old buildings near the center—an old hotel (now a pub) decorated with wrought-iron porches, a shire hall for government, and some attractive steepled churches. Amenities such as recreation complexes, hospitals, doctors, libraries, and schools are more abundant than in small-town America. Moreover, these towns are not dying, but remain vibrant, with thriving main streets and numerous children.

OUTBACK LIFE

The Outback is desert Australia. It differs in many ways from the Bush. People are few in number, and depopulation

"Queensland raised cottages," standing on piers above the ground, prevail in the northeast and demonstrate the special regional character of the tropical Australian bush.

has set in as a substantial number of residents depart for the Green Crescent. Most Euro-Australians who remain behind work in the mining and tourism industries. A huge part of the Outback is not used even for livestock ranching.

Increasingly, the Outback is becoming again a land of the Aborigines. These original Australians now control huge parts of the Outback and even some of its mineral wealth. "Anglo-Celtic" really cannot correctly describe the culture here. Perhaps "Euro-Aboriginal" would be better. Again, several Australias seem to exist.

In the future, Australia will have to face several major challenges, including assimilating its new multicultural population and maintaining its wealth and high standard of living.

7

The Australian Future

Predicting the future is a hazardous business at best. Too many unpredictable things happen. History is essentially a series of connected accidents. But a good place to begin would be with a brief overview of what we know of Australia as this new century begins.

A SUMMARY

We have seen that Australia's natural habitat is diverse, combining arid and humid, mountain and plain, rain forest and desert. It is rich in minerals and poor in the amount of cropland.

Its settlement was equally diverse, both ancient and modern, Aboriginal and European, convict and free. Powerful human forces, however, also acted to unify—popular culture, mateship, language, the Anglo-Celtic culture, the political unity of the continent, the nationalism built of isolation, suffering, democracy, and pride.

Economic geography told of great regional variety in land use and industry. It also described the bases of a prosperous, even wealthy Australia.

If Australia faces problems in the future, they will not likely come from within.

TOWARD THE TWENTY-FIRST CENTURY

In 2000, Australians headed toward the coming twenty-first century by hosting the Summer Olympic Games in Sydney. What the world saw on television was a modern, prosperous, talented, creative, multicultural, easygoing, and tolerant people.

To these attributes it might be added that Aussies do not take themselves too seriously. They are hedonists—people devoted to having a pleasurable life. Australia has no aspirations to be a world power and rather enjoys being geographically on the outer edge of things.

THE MYTH OF INNOCENCE

Australia is deeply involved in world trade and the global economy. It was attacked by bombers during World War II and has participated in wars on three other continents. Terrorism has touched and killed many.

Even so, Aussies still feel far removed from the center of world events. They cherish, subconsciously at least, a myth of innocence and refuge. Remoteness, they feel, will shelter them from the turmoil and disasters of the modern world and the future. Emotionally, they are safe in the fortress of their continent-nation.

Rationally, they know better. One 1950s movie—*On the Beach*—should have shattered the myth of innocence. In that film, the United States and the Soviet Union engage in a nuclear war. A lethal cloud of radioactivity spreads slowly but inevitably across the Earth. Eventually, Australia is the last place where human life exists. Then, all the Aussies die, too, as their imaginary refuge is violated.

CHALLENGES

Armed with their virtues, attributes, and myths, Australians face several major challenges. One of these is assimilation. Having chosen the path of multiculturalism, Aussies can no longer fall back on the Anglo-Celtic culture that served so well for so long. A new national identity will need to be forged. "Mateship" might be expanded and revised in ways to accommodate the new multicultural population, just as it earlier united English, Irish, and Scot.

The second challenge, too, is an enduring one faced in earlier centuries—location. Geographic location cuts two ways. It makes it difficult for Australia to engage in foreign trade and to attract tourists. Even from the perspective of Asia, Australia lies on the periphery. But location also places Australia next door to one of the densely settled and most deeply troubled countries of the world—Indonesia.

Indonesia

Indonesia, in fact, is the most unpredictable factor in Australia's future. It is a country of almost countless islands, with about 230 million inhabitants. Indonesia is the largest Muslim country in the world. It is plagued by civil wars, terrorism, and deep economic troubles. Indonesia could easily collapse and fragment, amid chaos and warfare. One splinter, East Timor, has already seceded.

Australia, a scant 290 miles (467 kilometers) from the nearest Indonesian isles, would feel the consequences of that country's collapse. Refugees by the millions could come. Trade routes could become mine-strewn and pirate-infested. Islamic terrorism could leap from Bali to the Australian continent.

Staying Rich

The biggest future challenge of all for Australia will be to maintain its wealth and high standard of living. This challenge is interwoven with those of location and Indonesia.

The attributes and virtues of the Aussies prepare them well to face all the challenges, though. They will need their irreverent sense of humor, their lack of pretension and pomposity, their creativity and talent, their multicultural diversity, their grit, spirit, pride, and rough-and-ready attitude.

Land area	approx. 2.9 million square miles (approx. 4.8 million square kilometers)
Population, 2002	approx. 19.6 million
Total Fertility Rate (TFR)	1.7
Rate of Natural Increase of Population	+0.6 percent per year
Infant Mortality Rate	5.2
Percentage of population	
Under 15 years of age	20 percent
Over 65 years of age	12 percent
Average life expectancy	80 years
Percentage of population living in urban areas	85 percent
Percentage of population foreign-born, 2000	24 percent
Percentage of land forested	5.3 percent
Percentage of land cultivated	6 percent
Percentage of land in pasture	55 percent
Capital city	Canberra
Government	parliamentary democracy
Head of state	prime minister
Role of British monarch	ceremonial head of state of Australia, represented by a resident governor general
Status in British Commonwealth	a member commonwealth
Currency	Australian dollar (in October 2002, $1.00 American = $1.82 Australian)

History at a Glance

50,000 B.C.	Approximate time of arrival of the first Aborigines.
A.D. 1616	Dutch ships arrive, beginning three decades of exploration by the Netherlands.
1688	English explorer William Dampier reaches Australia.
1770	Englishman James Cook's voyage of exploration turns British attention to Australia as a possible settlement site.
1788	British settlement begins, with the founding of Sydney and the colony of New South Wales by largely English convicts.
1801–03	Matthew Flinders circumnavigates Australia, carefully mapping the entire coastline.
1803	First British settlement in Tasmania.
1827–1829	First British settlements in Western Australia, at Albany (1827) and at Perth (1829); the colony was called Swanland at the time.
1835	Melbourne founded, and with it, the colony of Victoria.
1836	Founding of Adelaide and the colony of South Australia.
1838	First German settlers in Australia arrive in the Barossa Valley of South Australia.
1842	First permanent settlement at Brisbane, the beginning of the colony of Queensland.
1842	Copper first discovered, hinting at Australia's mineral wealth.
1847	First Barossa Valley winery opens.
1851	Gold first discovered, prompting a gold rush to Australia and the discovery of other gold mines; rapid population growth was one result.
1860–1862	First two overland crossings of the continent, from south to north.
1860s	Shipments of convicts to Australia ends; by then the huge majority of immigrants were "free" settlers.
1880	"Bushranger" gang leader Ned Kelly executed, ending a period of lawlessness on the settlement frontier; Kelly becomes a folk hero to many, especially those of convict or Irish origin.
1901	Commonwealth of Australia established as an independent country within the British Empire.
1901–1927	Capital of Australia is Melbourne.
1908	The site for the future national capital, Canberra, is chosen.

1915–1916	Very large numbers of Australian soldiers die near Gallipoli in the Dardanelles Campaign of World War I, fighting against the Turks; the losses are so huge as to help define Australian nationalism.
1927	Canberra replaces Melbourne as the capital of Australia.
1942	Japanese bomb Darwin and several other northern towns.
1945	Campaign begins to recruit white immigrants from the war-torn European mainland, prompting Italians, Greeks, and Serbs, in particular, to come.
1956	Summer Olympic Games held at Melbourne – Australia's "debut" as a major country.
1970s	Australia opens immigration to nonwhites for the first time, particularly to Asians.
1999	Vote on Australia leaving the British Empire, renouncing the royal family, and becoming a republic – the majority votes to keep things as they are.
2000	Summer Olympic Games at Sydney reveal Australia to be a progressive, beautiful, and talented country.
2002	October 12: An Islamic terrorist bomb explodes in the resort of Kuta, on the island of Bali, Indonesia, killing more than 80 Australian tourists.

Glossary

Aborigines: The original, pre-European people of Australia, present for perhaps as long as 50,000 years.

antipodes: The opposite side of the Earth; for the British Isles, Australia lies at the antipodes.

Artesian: Subsurface water under pressure that flows to the surface without pumping when a well is drilled, as in Australia's Great Artesian Basin.

Aussie: Nickname for an Australian.

billabong: A broad, flat valley in the dry part of Australia that fills with water during rainy spells.

boomerang: A curved piece of wood used by Aborigines in hunting; it is a thrown weapon that has the unique property of returning in flight to the thrower, should it miss its target.

Bush: A rural area, generally one with farms, ranches, and small towns.

bushfire: A wildfire raging through the brush and forests of the Bush.

bushranger: An outlaw of the Bush country in frontier time.

Cockney: The nasal English dialect of London's lower classes that became, with modifications, the national dialect of Australia.

deindustrialization: The relative decline of manufacturing in Australia beginning about 1980.

didgeridoo: A unique woodwind musical instrument invented by the Aborigines and now part of Australian popular culture.

dingo: A feral predator dog of Australia descended from the domestic dogs that accompanied the ancient Aboriginal colonization of Australia.

eucalyptus: The dominant genus of trees and shrubs in the forests and brush lands of Australia; a "gum" tree.

First Fleeters: The convicts on the first fleet of ships sent to Australia in 1788.

governor general: Official appointed by the queen or king of England to act as his or her official authority in Australia.

Green Crescent: The crescent-shaped zone of moist climates that flanks Australia's dry lands on the south, east, and north.

Green Triangle: A vernacular region in far southeastern South Australia and the most humid part of that state.

Gross Domestic Product (GDP): The value of all goods and services produced in Australia in a year.

infant mortality rate: The number of infants per 1,000 live births each year who die before reaching one year of age.

Kata Tjuta (The Olgas): A remarkable sandstone rock cluster standing above the Western Plateau near Uluru in the Northern Territory.

low sun: In tropical Australia, the season when the noon sun is lowest on the horizon; the tropical equivalent of winter.

marsupials: A diverse family of mammals most common to Australia, including kangaroos, koalas, and many others.

mateship: The close bond forged among convicts from the British Isles in early Australia, weakening the differences among the English, Irish, and Scots and helping early on to forge an Anglo-Celtic identity unique to Australia.

New Zealanders: Nicknamed "Kiwis," the second largest immigrant group in Australia in 2000.

Nullarbor: A vast treeless expanse of territory in the southern reaches of the Western Plateau.

Outback: In one sense, all of rural Australia, but more normally used to describe the desert and semi-desert heart of Australia.

Oz: A nickname for Australia contracted and corrupted from "Aus" and influenced by the movie, *The Wizard of Oz.*

Red Centre: Name sometimes used by Aussies to describe the desert core of their country; same as "Red Heart."

Red Heart: *See* Red Centre.

roundabout: A traffic circle, widely used in Australia in place of traffic lights.

Royal Flying Doctor Service: A system by which doctors fly in small aircraft to remote places in the Bush and Outback to care for patients.

sheila: Australian slang word meaning "woman;" men are called "blokes."

station: The Australian word for "ranch."

Stone Age: Older cultures that do not engage in metalworking, as was true of the Aborigines.

Glossary

Tassie: A nickname for Tasmania.

Taswegian: A resident of Tasmania.

Torres Strait Islanders: Native population of a series of small Australian-owned islands lying between the northern tip of Queensland and the country of Papua New Guinea.

total fertility rate (TFR): The average number of children born to women in a population during their lifetime.

Tropic of Capricorn: The parallel of latitude at 23 1/2° South of the equator that marks the border between the tropics and the mid-latitudes; it passes through the middle of Australia, so that nearly half of the continent lies in the tropics.

Uluru (Ayers Rock): The world's largest sandstone monolith towering over the Western Plateau in the southwestern part of Australia's Northern Territory; a place sacred to the Aborigines.

Vegemite: Salty spread happily consumed by Aussies on bread or just about anything edible.

Allen, H. C. *Bush and Backwoods: A Comparison of the Frontier in Australia and the United States.* Sydney: Angus & Robertson, 1959.

Bryson, Bill. *In a Sunburned Country.* New York: Broadway Books, 2000.

Camm, Jack C. R., John McQuilton, Trevor W. Plumb, and Steven G. Yorke. *Australians: A Historical Atlas.* Broadway, New South Wales: Fairfax, Syme & Weldon, 1987.

Coppell, Bill. *Australia in Facts and Figures.* Ringwood, Victoria: Penguin Books, 1994.

Dixson, Miriam. *The Imaginary Australian: Anglo-Celts and Identity, 1788 to the Present.* Sydney: University of New South Wales Press, 1999.

Goldberg, S. L., and F. B. Smith. *Australian Cultural History.* Cambridge: Cambridge University Press, 1988.

Greiner, Alyson L., and Terry G. Jordan-Bychkov. *Anglo-Celtic Australia: Colonial Immigration and Cultural Regionalism.* Santa Fe, NM and Harrisonburg, VA: Center for American Places, 2003.

Griffin, Trevor, and Murray McCaskill, eds. *Atlas of South Australia.* Adelaide: South Australian Government Printing Division and Wakefield Press, 1986.

Hardjono, Ratih. *The White Tribe of Asia.* Clayton, Victoria: Monash University Asia Institute, 1992.

Harriman, R. J., and E. S. Clifford, eds. *Atlas of New South Wales.* Sydney: Central Mapping Authority of New South Wales, 1987.

Hughes, Robert. *The Fatal Shore: The Epic of Australia's Founding.* New York: Vintage Books, 1988.

Jarvis, Neil, ed. *Western Australia: An Atlas of Human Endeavor,* 2nd ed. Perth: Western Australia Department of Lands and Surveys, 1986.

Jupp, James, ed. *The Australian People: An Encyclopedia of the Nation, Its People and Their Origins.* North Ryde, New South Wales: Angus & Robertson, 1988.

Lucas, David. *The Welsh, Irish, Scots, and English in Australia: A Demographic Profile with Statistical Appendix.* Canberra: Australian Institute of Multicultural Affairs, 1987.

Meinig, Donald W. *On the Margins of the Good Earth: The South Australian Wheat Frontier.* Chicago: Association of American Geographers and Rand McNally, 1962.

Bibliography

Paul, Erik C. *Australia: Too Many People?* Aldershot, England: Ashgate, 2002.

Powell, Joseph M. *An Historical Geography of Modern Australia.* Cambridge: Cambridge University Press, 1988.

Robson, L. L. *The Convict Settlers of Australia,* 2nd ed. Carlton, Victoria: Melbourne University Press, 1994.

Spate, Oskar H. K. *Australia.* London: Ernest Benn, 1968.

Stratford, Elaine. *Australian Cultural Geographies.* South Melbourne, Victoria: Oxford University Press, 1999.

Taylor, Griffith. "The Frontiers of Settlement in Australia." *Geographical Review,* 1926, 16: pp. 1–25.

Theophanous, Andrew C. *Understanding Multiculturalism and Australian Identity.* Melbourne: Elikia Books, 1995.

2002 Year Book Australia. Canberra, Australian Capital Territory: Australian Bureau of Statistics.

Ward, Russel B. *The Australian Legend.* Melbourne: Oxford University Press, 1958.

White, Richard. *Inventing Australia: Images and Identity, 1688–1980.* Sydney: George Allen & Union, 1981.

Index

Index

Picture Credits

TERRY G. JORDAN-BYCHKOV is the Walter Prescott Webb Professor in the Department of Geography at the University of Texas at Austin. A native of Dallas and a sixth-generation Texan, he earned his doctorate in cultural and historical geography at the University of Wisconsin at Madison. He has served as honorary president of the Association of American geographers and received an Honors Award from that professional organization. Professor Jordan-Bychkov has been listed in *Who's Who in America* since 1987. His main research interest has been in European culture and its transfer to overseas lands. He is author or coauthor of over 25 books and more than 100 scholarly articles. These include *The Human Mosaic: A Thematic Introduction to Human Geography*, 9th edition (W.H. Freeman); *The European Culture Area*, 4th edition (Rowman & Littlefield); *Anglo-Celtic Australia: Colonial Immigration and Cultural Regionalism* (2002); *The Upland South: The Making of an American Folk Region and Landscape* (2003). His hobbies are genealogy and travel, and he has visited 64 different countries.

CHARLES F. ("FRITZ") GRITZNER is Distinguished Professor of Geography at South Dakota University in Brookings. He is now in his fifth decade of college teaching and research. During his career, he has taught more than 60 different courses, spanning the fields of physical, cultural, and regional geography. In addition to his teaching, he enjoys writing, working with teachers, and sharing his love for geography with students. As consulting editor for the MODERN WORLD NATIONS series, he has a wonderful opportunity to combine each of these "hobbies." Fritz has served as both president and executive director of the National Council for Geographic Education and has received the Council's highest honor, the George J. Miller Award for Distinguished Service.

DATE DUE

994
Jordan-Bychkov
Jordan-Bychkov, Terry G.
Australia